A Day's Tour

By

Percy Hetherington Fitzgerald

Edition : Culturea (culurea.fr), 34 Hérault
Contact : infos@culturea.fr
Impression : BOD, Norderstedt (Allemagne)
ISBN : 9791041981533
Date de publication : juillet 2023
Mise en page et maquettage : https://reedsy.com/
Cet ouvrage a été composé avec la police Bauer Bodoni

A DAY'S TOUR.

I.

IN TOWN.

It is London, of a bright sultry August day, when the flags seem scorching to the feet, and the sun beats down fiercely. It has yet a certain inviting attraction. There is a general air of bustle, and the provincial, trundled along in his cab, his trunks over his head, looks out with a certain awe and sense of delight, noting, as he skirts the Park, the gay colours glistening among the dusty trees, the figures flitting past, the riders, the carriages, all suggesting a foreign capital. The great city never looks so brilliant or so stately as on one of these 'broiling' days. One calls up with a sort of wistfulness the great and picturesque cities abroad, with their grand streets and palaces, ever a delightful novelty. We long to be away, to be crossing over that night—enjoying a cool fresh passage, all troubles and monotony left behind.

On one such day this year—a Wednesday—these mixed impressions and longings presented themselves with unwonted force and iteration. So wistful and sudden a craving for snapping all ties and hurrying away was after all spasmodic, perhaps whimsical; but it was quickened by that sultry, melting air of the parks and the tropical look of the streets. The pavements seemed to glare fiercely like furnaces; there was an air of languid Eastern enjoyment. The very dogs 'snoozed' pleasantly in shady corners, and all seemed happy as if enjoying a holiday.

How delightful and enviable those families—the father, mother, and fair daughters, now setting off gaily with their huge boxes—who to-morrow would be beside the ever-delightful Rhine, posting on to Cologne and Coblentz. What a welcome ring in those names! Stale, hackneyed as it is, there comes a thrill as we get the first glimpse of the silvery placid waters and their majestic windings. Even the hotels, the bustle, and the people, holiday and festive, all seem novel and gay. With some people this fairy look of things foreign never 'stales,' even with repetition. It is as with the illusions of the stage, which in some natures will triumph over the rudest, coarsest shocks.

Well, that sweltering day stole by. The very cabmen on their 'stands' nodded in blissful dreams. The motley colours in the Park—a stray cardinal-coloured parasol or two added to the effect—glinted behind the trees. The image of the happy tourists in the foreign streets grew more vivid. The restlessness increased every hour, and was not to be 'laid.'

Living within a stone's-throw of Victoria Station, I find a strange and ever new sensation in seeing the night express and its passengers starting for foreign lands—some wistful and anxious, others supremely happy. It is next in interest to the play. The carriages are marked 'CALAIS,' 'PARIS,' etc. It is even curious to think that, within three hours or so, they will be on foreign soil, among the French spires, sabots, blouses, gendarmes, etc. These are trivial and fanciful notions, but help to fortify what one has of the little faiths of life, and what one wise man, at least, has said: that it is the smaller unpretending things of life that make up its pleasures, particularly those that come unexpectedly, and from which we hope but little.

When all these thoughts were thus tumultuously busy, an odd bizarre idea presented itself. By an unusual concatenation, there was before me but a strictly-tightened space of leisure that could not be expanded. Friday must be spent at home. This was Wednesday, already three-quarters spent; but there was the coming night and the whole of Thursday. But Friday morning imperatively required that the traveller should be found back at home again. The whole span, theirreducible maximum, not to be stretched by any contrivance beyond about thirty hours. Something could be done, but not much. As I thought of the strict and narrow limits, it seemed that these were some precious golden hours, and never to recur again; the opportunity must be seized, or lost for ever! As I walked the sunshiny streets, images rose of the bright streets abroad, their quaint old towers, and town-halls, and marketplaces, and churches, red-capped fisherwomen—all this scenery was 'set,'—properties and decorations—and the foreign play seemed to open before my eyes and invite me.

There is an Eastern story of a man who dipped his head into a tub of water, and who there and then mysteriously passed through a long series of events: was married, had children, saw them grow up, was taken prisoner by barbarians, confined long in gaol, was finally tried, sentenced, and led out to execution, with the scimitar about to descend, when of a sudden—he drew his head out of the water. And lo! all these marvels had passed in a second! What if there were to be magically crowded into those few hours all that could possibly be seen—sea and land, old towns in different countries, strange people, cathedrals, town-halls, streets, etc.? It would be like some wild, fitful dream. And on the Friday I would draw my head, as it were, out of the tub. But it would need the nicest balancing and calculation, not a minute to be lost, everything to be measured and jointed together beforehand.

There was something piquant in this notion. Was not life short? and precious hours were too often wasted carelessly and dawdled away. It might even be worth while to see how much could be seen in these few hours. In a few moments the resolution was taken, and I was walking down to Victoria, and in two hours was in Snargate Street, Dover.

II.

DOVER.

Dover has an old-fashioned dignity of its own; the town, harbour, ports, and people seem, as it were, consecrated to packets. There is an antique and reverend grayness in its old inns, old streets, old houses, all clustered and huddled into the little sheltered amphitheatre, as if trying to get down close by their pride, the packets. For centuries it has been the threshold, the hall-door, of England. It is the last inn, as it were, from which we depart to see foreign lands. History, too, comes back on us: we think of 'expresses' in fast sloops or fishing-boats; of landings at Dover, and taking post for London in war-time; how kings have embarked, princesses disembarked—all in that awkward, yet snug harbour. A most curious element in this feeling is the faint French flavour reaching across—by day the white hills yonder, by night the glimmering lights on the opposite coast. The inns, too, have a nautical, seaport air, running along the beach, as they should do, and some of the older ones having a bulging stern-post look about their lower windows. Even the frowning, fortress-like coloured pile, the Lord Warden, thrusts its shoulders forward on the right, and advances well out into the sea, as if to be the first to attract the arrivals. There is a quaint relish, too, in the dingy, old-fashioned marine terrace of dirty tawny brick, its green verandas and jalousies, which lend quite a tropical air. Behind them, in shelter, are little dark squares, of a darker stone, with glimpses of the sea and packets just at the corners. Indeed, at every point wherever there is a slit or crevice, a mast or some cordage is sure to show itself, reminding us how much we are of the packet, packety. Ports of this kind, with all their people and incidents, seem to be devised for travellers; with their flaring lights, up-all-nighthotels, the railway winding through the narrow streets, the piers, the stormy waters, the packets lying by all the piers and filling every convenient space. The old Dover of Turner's well-known picture, or indeed of twenty years ago, with its 'dumpy' steamers, its little harbour, and rude appliances for travel, was a very different Dover from what it is now. There was then no rolling down in luxurious trains to an Admiralty Pier. The stoutest heart might shrink, or at least feel dismally uncomfortable, as he found himself discharged from the station near midnight of a blowy, tempestuous night, and saw his effects shouldered by a porter, whom he was invited to follow down to the pier, where the funnel of the 'Horsetend' or Calais boat is moaning dismally. Few lights were twinkling in the winding old-fashioned streets; but the near vicinity of ocean was felt uncomfortably in harsh blasts and whistling sounds. The little old harbour, like that of some fishing-place, offered scarcely any room. The much-buffeted steamer lay bobbing and springing at its moorings, while a dingy oil-lamp marked the gangway. A comforting welcome awaited us from some old salt, who uttered the cheering announcement that it was 'agoin' to be a roughish night.'

On this night there was an entertainment announced at the 'Rooms,' and to pass away the time I looked in. It was an elocutionist one, entitled 'Merry-Making Moments, or, Spanker's Wallet of Varieties,' with a portrait of Spanker on the bills opening the wallet with an expression of delight or surprise. This was his 'Grand Competition Night,' when a 'magnificent goblet' was competed for by all comers, which I had already seen in a shop window, a blue ribbon reposing in dégagé fashion across it. If a tumbler of the precious metal could be called a magnificent goblet—it was scarcely bigger—it deserved the title. The poor operator was declaiming as I entered, in unmistakable Scotch, the history of 'Little Breeches,' and giving it with due pathos. I am bound to say that a sort of balcony which hung out at the end was well filled by the unwashed takers, or at least donees, of sixpenny tickets. There was a purpose in this, as will be seen. After being taken through 'The Raven,' and 'The Dying Burglar,' the competition began. This was certainly the most diverting portion of the entertainment, from its genuineness, the eagerness of the competitors, and their ill-disguised jealousy. There were four candidates. A doctor-looking man with a beard, and who had the air either of reading familiar prayers to his household with good parsonic effect, or of having tried the stage, uttered his lines with a very superior air, as though the thing were not in doubt. Better than he, however, was one, probably a draper's assistant, who competed with a wild and panting fashion, tossing his arms, now raising, now dropping his voice, and every h, too. But a shabby man, who looked as if he had once practised tailoring, next stepped on the platform, and at once revealed himself as the local poet. Encouraged by the generous applause, he announced that he would recite some lines 'he 'ad wrote on the great storm which committed such 'avoc on hour pier.' There were local descriptions, and local names, which always touched the true chord. Notably an allusion to a virtuous magnate then, I believe, at rest:

'Amongst the var'ous noble works,It should be widely known,'Twas WILLIAM BROWN' (applause) 'that gave this townThe Dover's Sailors' 'OME!' (applause).

Need I say that when the votes came to be taken, this poet received the cup? His joy and mantling smiles I shall not forget, though the donor gave it to him with unconcealed disgust; it showed what universal suffrage led to. The doctor and the other defeated candidates, who had been asked to retire to a private room during the process of decision, were now obliged to emerge in mortified procession, there being no other mode of egress. The doctor's face was a study. The second part was to follow. But it was now growing late, and time and mail-packets wait for no man.

III.

THE PACKET.

As I come forth from the Elocution Contest, I find that night has closed in. Not a ripple is on the far-stretching blue waste. From the high cliffs that overhang the town and its amphitheatre can be seen the faintly outlined harbour, where the white-chimneyed packet snoozes as it were, the smoke curling upwards, almost straight. The sea-air blows fresh and welcome, though it does not beat on a 'fevered brow.' There is a busy hum and clatter in the streets, filled with soldiers and sailors and chattering sojourners. Now do the lamps begin to twinkle lazily. There is hardly a breath stirring, and the great chalk-cliffs gleam out in a ghostly fashion, like mammoth wave-crests.

As it draws on to ten o'clock, the path to the Admiralty Pier begins to darken with flitting figures hurrying down past the fortress-like Lord Warden, now ablaze and getting ready its hospice for the night; the town shows itself an amphitheatre of dotted lights—while down below white vapours issue walrus-like from the sonorous 'scrannel-pipes' of the steamer. Gradually the bustle increases, and more shadowy figures come hurrying down, walking behind their baggage trundled before them. Now a faint scream, from afar off inland, behind the cliffs, gives token that the trains, which have been tearing headlong down from town since eight o'clock, are nearing us; while the railway-gates fast closed, and porters on the watch with green lamps, show that the expresses are due. It is a rather impressive sight to wait at the closed gates of the pier and watch these two outward-bound expresses arrive. After a shriek, prolonged and sustained, the great trains from Victoria and Ludgate, which met on the way and became one, come thundering on, the enormous and powerful engine glaring fiercely, flashing its lamps, and making the pier tremble. Compartment after compartment of first-class carriages flit by, each lit up so refulgently as to show the crowded passengers, with their rugs and bundles dispersed about them. It is a curious change to see the solitary pier, jutting out into the waves, all of a sudden thus populated with grand company, flashing lights, and saloon-like splendour—ambassadors, it may be, generals for the seat of war, great merchants like the Rothschilds, great singers or actors, princes, dukes, millionnaires, orators, writers, 'beauties,' brides and bridegrooms, all ranged side by side in those cells, or vis-à-vis. That face under the old-fashioned travelling-cap may be that of a prime minister, and that other gentlemanly person a swindling bank-director flying from justice.

During the more crowded time of the travelling season it is not undramatic, and certainly entertaining, to stand on the deck of the little boat, looking up at the vast pier and platform some twenty or thirty feet above one's head, and see the flood of passengers descending in ceaseless procession; and more wonderful still, the baggage being hurled down the 'shoots.' On nights of pressure this may take nearly an hour, and yet not a second appears to be lost. One gazes in wonder at the vast brass-bound chests swooping down and caught so deftly by the nimble mariners; the great black-domed ladies' dress-baskets and boxes; American and French trunks, each with its national mark on it. Every instant the pile is growing. It seems like building a mansion with vast blocks of stone piled up on each other. Hat-boxes and light leather cases are sent bounding down like footballs, gradually and by slow degrees forming the mountain.

What secrets in these chests! what tales associated with them! Bridal trousseaux, jewels, letters, relics of those loved and gone; here the stately paraphernalia of a family assumed to be rich and prosperous, who in truth are in flight, hurrying away with their goods. Here, again, the newly bought 'box' of the bride, with her initials gaudily emblazoned; and the showy, glittering chests of the Americans.

There is a physiognomy in luggage, distinct as in clothes; and a strange variety, not uninteresting. How significant, for instance, of the owner is the weather-beaten, battered old portmanteau of the travelling bachelor, embrowned with age, out of shape, yet still strong and serviceable!—a business-like receptacle, which, like him, has travelled thousands of miles, been rudely knocked about, weighed, carried hither and thither, encrusted with the badges of hotels as an old vessel is with barnacles, grim and reserved like its master, and never lost or gone astray.

Now the engines and their trains glide away home. The shadowy figures stand round in crowds. To the reflecting mind there is something bewildering and even mournful in the survey of this huge agglomeration and of its owners, the muffled, shadowy figures, some three hundred in number, grouped together, and who will be dispersed again in a few hours.

A yacht-voyage could not be more tranquilly delightful than this pleasant moonlight transit. We are scarcely clear of the twinkling lights of the Dover amphitheatre, grown more and more distant, when those of the opposite coast appear to draw near and yet nearer. Often as one has crossed, the sense of a new and strange impression is never wanting. The sense of calm and silence, the great waste of sea, the monotonous 'plash' of the paddle-wheels, the sort of solitude in the midst of such a crowd, the gradually lengthening distance behind, with the lessening, as gradual, in front, and the always novel feeling of approach to a new country—these elements impart a sort of dreamy, poetical feeling to the scene. Even the calm resignation of the wrapped-up shadows seated in a sort of retreat, and devoted to their own thoughts or slumbers, add to this effect. With which comes the thought of the brave little vessels, which through day and night, year after year, dance over these uncertain waters in 'all weathers,' as it is termed. When the night is black as Erebus, and the sea in its fury boiling and raging over the pier, the Lord Warden with its storm-shutters up, and timid guests removed to more sheltered quarters, the very stones of the pier shaken from their places by the violence of the monster outside—the little craft, wrapping its mantle about its head, goes out fearlessly, and, emerging from the harbour to be flung about, battered with wild fury, forces her way on through the night, which its gallant sailors call, with truth, 'an awful one.'

While busy with these thoughts I take note of a little scene of comedy, or perhaps of a farcical kind, which is going on near me, in which two 'Harrys' of the purest kind were engaged, and whose oddities lightened the tediousness of the passage. One had seen foreign parts, and was therefore regarded with reverence by his companion.

They were promenading the deck, and the following dialogue was borne to me in snatches:

First Harry (interrogatively, and astonished): 'Eh? no! Now, really?'

Second Harry: 'Oh, Lord bless yer, yes! It comes quite easy, you know' (or 'yer know'). 'A little trouble at first; but, Lord bless yer' (this benediction was imparted many times during the conversation), 'it ain't such a difficult thing at all.'

I now found they were speaking of acquiring the French language—a matter the difficulty of which they thought had been absurdly overrated. Then the second Harry: 'Of course it is! Suppose you're in a Caffy, and want some wine; you just call to the waiter, and you say—'

First Harry (who seems to think that the secret has already been communicated): 'Dear me; yes, to be sure—to be sure! I never thought of that. A Caffy?'

Second Harry: 'Oh, Lor' bless yer, it comes as easy as—that! Well, you go say to the fellow—just as you would say to an English waiter—"Don-ny maw"—(pause)—"dee Vinne."'

First Harry (amazed): 'So that's the way! Dear, dear me! Vinne!'

Second Harry: 'O' course it is the way! Suppose you want yer way to the railway, you just go ask for the "Sheemin—dee—Fur." Fur, you know, means "rail" in French—Sheemin is "the road," you know.'

Again lost in wonder at the simplicity of what is popularly supposed to be so thorny, the other Harry could only repeat:

'So that's it! What is it, again? Sheemin—'

'Sheemin dee Fur.'

Later, in the fuss and bustle of the 'eating hall,' this 'Harry,' more obstreperous than ever by contact with the foreigners, again attracted my attention. Everywhere I heard his voice; he was rampant.

'When the chap laid hold of my bag, "Halloo," says I; "hands off, old boy," says I.

"'Eel Fo!" says he.

"'Eel-pie!" says I. "Blow your Fo," says I, and didn't he grin like an ape? I declare I thought I'd have split when he came again with his "Eel Fo!"'

He was then in his element. Everything new to him was 'a guy,' or 'so rum,' or 'the queerest go you ever.' One of the two declared that, 'in all his experience and in all his life he had never heard sich a lingo as French;' and further, that 'one of their light porters at Bucklersbury would eat half a dozen of them Frenchmen for a bender.'

This strange, grotesque dialogue I repeat textually almost; and, it may be conceived, it was entertaining in a high degree. 'Sheemin dee Fur' was the exact phonetic pronunciation, and the whole scene lingers pleasantly in the memory.

IV.

CALAIS.

But it is now close on midnight, and we are drawing near land; the eye of the French phare grows fiercer and more glaring, until, close on midnight, the traveller finds the blinding light flashed full on him, as the vessel rushes past the wickerwork pier-head. One or two beings, whose unhappy constitution it is to be miserable and wretched at the very whisper of the word 'SEA,' drag themselves up from below, rejoicing that here isCALAIS. Beyond rises the clustered town confined within its walls. As we glide in between the friendly arms of the openwork pier, the shadowy outlines of the low-lying town take shape and enlarge, dotted with lamps as though pricked over with pin-holes. The fiery clock of the station, that sits up all night from year's end to year's end; the dark figures with tumbrils, and a stray coach waiting; the yellow gateway and drawbridge of the fortress just beyond, and the chiming of carillons in a wheezy fashion from the old watch-tower within, make up a picture.

Such, indeed, it used to be—not without its poetry, too; but the old Calais days are gone. Now the travellers land far away down the pier, at the new-fangled 'Calais Maritime,' forsooth! and do not even approach the old town. The fishing-boats, laid up side by side along the piers, are shadowy. It seems a scene in a play. The great sea is behind us and all round. It is a curious feeling, thinking of the nervous unrest of the place, that has gone on for a century, and that will probably go on for centuries more. Certainly, to a person who has never been abroad, this midnight scene would be a picture not without a flavour of romance. But such glimpses of poetry are held intrusive in these matter-of-fact days.

There is more than an hour to wait, whilst the passengers gorge in the huge salle, and the baggage is got ashore. So I wander away up to the town.

How picturesque that stroll! Not wholly levelled are the old yellow walls; the railway-station with its one eye, and clock that never sleeps, opens its jaws with a cheerful bright light, like an inn fire; dark figures in cowls, soldiers, sailors, flit about; curiously-shaped tumbrils for the baggage lie up in ordinary. Here is the old arched gate, ditch, and drawbridge; Hogarth's old bridge and archway, where he drew the 'Roast Beef of Old England.' Passing over the bridge into the town unchallenged, I find a narrow street with yellow houses—the white shutters, the porches, the first glance of which affects one so curiously and reveals France. Here is the Place of Arms in the centre, whence all streets radiate. What more picturesque scene!—the moon above, the irregular houses straggling round, the quaint old town-hall, with its elegant tower, and rather wheezy but most musical chimes; its neighbour, the black, solemn watch-tower, rising rude and abrupt, seven centuries old, whence there used to be strict look-out for the English. Down one of these side streets is a tall building, with its long rows of windows and shutters and closed door (Quillacq's, now Dessein's), once a favourite house—the 'Silver Lion,' mentioned in the old memoirs, visited by Hogarth, and where, twenty years ago, there used to be a crowd of guests. Standing in the centre, I note a stray roysterer issuing from some long-closedcafé, hurrying home, while the carillons in their airy rococo-looking tower play their melodious tunes in a wheezy jangle that is interesting and novel. This chime has a celebrity in this quarter of France. I stayed long in the centre of that solitary place, listening to that midnight music.

It is a curious, not unromantic feeling, that of wandering about a strange town at midnight, and the effect increases as, leaving the place, I turn down a little by-street—the Rue de Guise—closed at the end by a beautiful building or fragment, unmistakably English in character. Behind it spreads the veil of blue sky, illuminated by the moon, with drifting white clouds passing lazily across. This is the entrance to the Hôtel de Guise—a gate-tower and archway, pure Tudor-English in character, and, like many an old house in the English counties, elegant and almost piquant in its design. The arch is flanked by slight hexagonal tourelles, each capped by a pinnacle decorated with niches in front. Within is a little courtyard, and fragments of the building running round in the same Tudor style, but given up to squalor and decay, evidently let out to poor lodgers. This charming fragment excites a deep melancholy, as it is a neglected survival, and may disappear at any moment—the French having little interest in these English monuments, indeed, being eager to efface them when they can. It is always striking to see this on some tranquil night, as I do now—and Calais is oftenest seen at midnight—and think of the Earl of Warwick, the 'deputy,' and of the English wool-staple merchants who traded here. Here lodged Henry VIII. in 1520; and twelve years later Francis I., when on a visit to Henry, took up his abode in this palace.

Crossing the place again, I come on the grim old church, built by the English, where were married our own King Richard II. and Isabelle of Valois—a curious memory to recur as we listen to the 'high mass' of a Calais Sunday. But the author of 'Modern Painters' has furnished the old church with its best poetical interpretation. 'I cannot find words,' he says in a noble passage,' to express the intense pleasure I have always felt at first finding myself, after some prolonged stay in England, at the foot of the tower of Calais Church. The large neglect, the noble unsightliness of it, the record of its years, written so vividly, yet without sign of weakness or decay; its stern vastness and gloom, eaten away by the Channel winds, and overgrown with bitter sea-grass. I cannot tell half the strange pleasures and thoughts that come about me at the sight of the old tower.' Most interesting of all is the grim, rusted, and gaunt watch-tower, before alluded to, which rises out of a block of modern houses in the place itself. It can be seen afar off from the approaching vessel, and until comparatively late times this venerable servant had done the charity of lighthouse work for a couple of centuries at least.

But one of the pleasantest associations connected with the town was the old Dessein's Hotel, which had somehow an inexpressibly old-fashioned charm, for it had a grace like some disused château. Some of the prettiest passages in Sterne's writings are associated with this place. We see the figures of the monk, the well-known host, the lady and thepetit-maître: to say nothing of the old désobligeante. Even of late years it was impossible to look at the old building, which remained unchanged, without calling up the image of Mr. Sterne, and the curious airy conversation—sprinkled with what execrable French both in grammar and spelling!—that took place at the gate. An air of the old times pervaded it strongly: it was like opening an old garde de vin. You passed out of the place and found yourself in the

Rue Royale—newly named Rue Leveux—and there, Dessein's stood before you, with its long yellow wall, archway and spacious courts, on each side a number of quaint gables or mansardes, sharp-roofed. Over the wall was seen the foliage of tall and handsome trees. There is a coloured print representing this entrance, with the meeting of the 'little master' and the lady—painted by Leslie—and which gives a good idea of the place. In the last century the courtyard used to be filled with posting-carriages, and the well-known remise lay here in a corner. Behind the house stretched large, well-stocked gardens, with which the guests at the hotel used to be recreated; while at the bottom of the garden, but opening into another street, was the theatre, built by the original Dessein, belonging to the hotel, and still used. This garden was wild and luxuriant, the birds singing, while the courtyard was dusty and weed-grown.

This charming picture has ever been a captivating one for the traveller. It seemed like an old country-house transferred to town. There was something indescribable in the tranquil flavour of the place, its yellow gamboge tint alternated with green vineries, its spacious courtyard and handsome chambers. It was bound up with innumerable old associations. Thackeray describes, with an almost poetical affection and sympathy, the night he spent there. He called up the image of Sterne in his 'black satin smalls,' and talked with him. They used to show his room, regularly marked, as I have seen it, 'STERNES'S ROOM, NO. 31,' with its mezzotint, after Sir Joshua, hung over the chimney-piece. But this tradition received a shock some sixty years since. An inquisitive and sceptical traveller fancied he saw an inscription or date lurking behind the vine-leaves that so luxuriantly covered the old house, and sent up a man on a ladder to clear away the foliage. This operation led to the discovery of a tablet, dated two years too late for

the authenticity of the building in which 'Sterne's room' was. The waiter, however, in nowise disconcerted, said the matter could be easily 'arranged' by selecting another room in an unquestioned portion of the building! To make up, however, there was a room labelled 'SIR WALTER SCOTT'S

ROOM,' with his portrait; and of this there could be no reasonable question.

In later years it did not flourish much, but gently decayed. Everything seemed in a state of mild sleepy abandonment and decay till about the year 1861, when the Desseins gave over business. The town, much straitened for room, and cramped within its fortifications, had long been casting hungry eyes on this spacious area. Strange to say, even in the prosaic pages of our own 'Bradshaw,' the epitaph of 'old Dessein's' is to be read among its advertisements:

'CALAIS.

'HÔTEL DESSEIN.—L. Dessein, the proprietor, has the honour to inform his numerous patrons, and travellers in general, that after the 1st of January his establishment will be transferred to the Hôtel Quillacq, which has been entirely done up, and will take the name of HÔTEL DESSEIN. The premises of the old Hôtel Dessein having been purchased by the town of Calais, it ceases to be an Hôtel for Travellers.'

Still, in this new function it was 'old Dessein's,' and you were shown 'Sterne's room,' etc. I recall wandering through it of a holiday, surveying the usual museum specimens—the old stones, invariable spear-heads, stuffed animals; in short, the usual rather heterogeneous collection, made up of 'voluntary contributions,' prompted half by the vanity of the donor and half by his indifference to the objects presented. We had not, indeed, the 'old pump' or the parish stocks, as at Little Pedlington, but there were things as interesting. Here were a few old pictures given by the Government, and labelled in writing; the car of Blanchard's balloon, and a cutting from a newspaper describing his arrival; portraits of the 'Citizen King' in his white trousers; ditto of Napoleon III., name pasted over; the flagstone, with an inscription, celebrating the landing of Louis XVIII., removed from the pier—in deference to Republican sensitiveness—no doubt to be restored again in deference to monarchical feelings; and, of course, a number of the usual uninteresting cases containing white cards, and much cotton, pins, and insects, stuffed birds, and symmetrically-arranged dried specimens, the invariable Indian gourds, and arrows, and moccasins, which 'no gentlemanly collection should be without.' Never, during many a visit, did I omit wandering up to see this pleasing, old, but ghostly memorial. It may be conceived what a shock it was when, on a recent visit, I found it gone—razed—carted away. I searched and searched—fancied I had mistaken the street; but no! it was gone for ever. During M. Jules Ferry's last administration, when the rage for 'Communal schools' set in, this tempting site had been seized upon, the interesting old place levelled, and a factory-like red-brick pile rapidly erected in its place. It was impossible not to feel a pang at this discovery; I felt that Calais without its Dessein's had lost its charm. Madame Dessein, a grand-niece or nearly-related descendant of le grand Dessein, still directs at Quillacq's—a pleasing old lady.

There is still a half hour before me, while the gorgers in 'Maritime Calais' are busy feeding against time; and while I stand in the place, listening to the wheezy old chimes, I recall a pleasant excursion, and a holiday that was spent there, at the time when the annual fêtes were being celebrated. Never was there a brighter day: all seemed to be new, and the very quintessence of what was foreign—the gay houses of different heights and patterns were decked with streamers, their parti-coloured blinds, devices, and balconies running round the place, and furnishing gaudy detail. Here there used to be plenty of movement, when the Lafitte diligences went clattering by, starting for Paris, before the voracious railway marched victoriously in and swallowed diligence, horses, postilions—bells, boots and all! The gay crowd passing across the place was making for the huge iron-gray cathedral, quite ponderous and fortress-like in its character. Here is the grand messe going on, the Swiss being seen afar off, standing with his halbert under the great arch, while between, down to the door, are the crowded congregation and the convenient chairs. Overhead the ancient organ is pealing out with rich sound, while the sun streams in through the dim-painted glass on the old-fashioned costumes of the fish-women, just falling on their gold earrings en passant. There is a dreamy air about this function, which associated itself, in some strange way, with bygone days of childhood, and it is hard to think that about two or three hours before the spectator was in all the prose of London.

For those who love novel and picturesque memories or scenes, there are few things more effective or pleasant to think of than one of these Sunday mornings in a strange unfamiliar French town, when every corner, and every house and figure—welcome novelty!—are gay as the costumes and colours in an opera. The night before it was, perhaps, the horrors of the packet, the cribbing in the cabin, the unutterable squalor and roughness of all things, the lowest depth of hard, ugly prose, together with the rudest buffeting and agitation, and poignant suffering; but, in a few hours, what a 'blessed' change! Now there is the softness of a dream in the bright cathedral church crowded to the door, the rites and figures seen afar off, the fuming incense, the music, the architecture!

During these musings the fiercely glaring clock warns me that time is running out; but a more singular monitor is the great lighthouse which rises at the entrance of the town, and goes through its extraordinary, almost fiendish, performance all the night long. This is truly a phenomenon. Lighthouses are usually relegated to some pier-end, and display their gyrations to the congenial ocean. But conceive a monster of this sort almost in the town itself, revolving ceaselessly, flashing and flaring into every street and corner of a street, like some Patagonian policeman with a giant 'bull's-eye.' A more singular, unearthly effect cannot be conceived. Wherever I stand, in shadow or out of it, this sudden flashing pursues me. It might be called the 'Demon Lighthouse.' For a moment, in picturesque gloom, watching the shadows cast by the Hogarthian gateway, I may be thinking of our great English painter sitting sketching the lean Frenchwomen, noting, too, the portal where the English arms used to be, when suddenly the 'Demon Lighthouse' directs his glare full on me, describes a sweep, is gone, and all is dark again. It suggests the policeman going his rounds. How the exile forced to sojourn here must detest this obtrusive beacon of the first class! It must become maddening in time for the eyes. Even in bed it has the effect of mild sheet-lightning. Municipality of Calais! move it away at once to a rational spot—to the end of the pier, where a lighthouse ought to be.

V.

TOURNAY.

But now back to 'Maritime Calais,' down to the pier, where a strange busy contrast awaits us. All is now bustle. In the great 'hall' hundreds are finishing their 'gorging,' paying bills, etc., while on the platform the last boxes and chests are being tumbled into the waggons with the peculiar tumbling, crashing sound which is so foreign. Guards and officials in cloaks and hoods pace up and down, and are beginning to chant their favourite 'En voiture, messieurs!' Soon all are packed into their carriages, which in France always present an old-fashioned mail-coach air with their protuberant bodies and panels. By one o'clock the signal is given, the lights flash slowly by, and we are rolling away, off into the black night. 'Maritime Calais' is left to well-earned repose; but for an hour or so only, until the returning mail arrives, when it will wake up again—a troubled and troublous nightmare sort of existence. Now for a plunge into Cimmerian night, with that dull, sustained buzz outside, as of some gigantic machinery whirling round, which seems a sort of lullaby, contrived mercifully to make the traveller drowsy and enwrap him in gentle sleep. Railway sleeping is, after all, a not unrefreshing form of slumber. There is the grateful 'nod, nod, nodding,' with the sudden jerk of an awakening; until the nodding becomes more overpowering, and one settles into a deep and profound sleep. Ugh! how chilly it gets! And the machinery—or is it the sea?—still roaring in one's ear.

What, stopping! and by the roadside, it seems; the day breaking, the atmosphere cold, steel-blue, and misty. Rubbing the pane, a few surviving lights are seen twinkling—a picture surely something Moslem. For there, separated by low-lying fields, rise clustered Byzantine towers and belfries, with strangely-quaint German-looking spires of the Nuremberg pattern, but all dimly outlined and mysterious in their grayness.

There was an extraordinary and original feeling in this approach: the old fortifications, or what remained of them, rising before me; the gloom, the mystery, the widening streak of day, and perfect solitariness. As I admired the shadowy belfry which rose so supreme and asserted itself among the spires, there broke out of a sudden a perfect charivari of bells—jangling, chiming, rioting, from various churches, while amid all was conspicuous the deep, solemn BOOM! BOOM! like the slow baying of a hound.

It is five o'clock, but it might be the middle of the night, so dark is it. This magic city, which seems like one of those in Albert Dürer's cuts, rises at a distance as if within walls. I stand in the roadside alone, deserted, the sole traveller set down. The train has flown on into the night with a shriek. The sleepy porter wonders, and looks at me askance.

As I take my way from the station and gradually approach the city—for there is a broad stretch between it and the railway unfilled by houses—I see the striking and impressive picture growing and enlarging. The jangling and the solemn occasional boom still go on: meant to give note that the day is opening. Nothing more awe-inspiring or poetical can be conceived than this 'cock-crow' promenade. Here are little portals suddenly opening on the stage, with muffled figures darting out, and worthy Belgians tripping from their houses—betimes, indeed—and hurrying away to mass. Thus to make the acquaintance of that grandest and most astonishing of old cathedrals, is to do so under the best and most suitable conditions: very different from the guide and cicerone business, which belongs to later hours of the day. I stand in the open place, under its shadow, and lift my eyes with wonder to the amazing and crowded cluster of spires and towers: its antique air, and even look of shattered dilapidation showing that the restorer has not been at his work. There was no smugness or trimness, or spick-and-spanness, but an awful and reverent austerity. And with an antique appropriateness to its functions the Flemish women, crones and maidens, all in their becoming cashmere hoods, and cloaks, and neat frills, still hurry on to the old Dom. Near me rose the antique beffroi, from whose jaws still kept booming the old bell, with a fine clang, the same that had often pealed out to rouse the burghers to discord and tumult. It pealed on, hoarse and even cracked, but persistently melodious, disregarding the contending clamours of its neighbours, just as some old baritone of the opera, reduced and broken down, will exhibit his 'phrasing'—all that is left to him. Quaint old burgher city, indeed, with the true flavour, though beshrew them for meddling with the fortifications!

That little scene in this place of Tournay is always a pleasant, picturesque memory.

I entered with the others. Within the cathedral was the side chapel, with its black oak screen, and a tawny-cheeked Belgian priest at the altar beginning the mass. Scattered round and picturesquely grouped were the crones and maidens aforesaid, on their wicker-chairs. A few surviving lamps twinkled fitfully, and shadowy figures crossed as if on the stage. But aloft, what an overpowering immensity, all vaulted shadows, the huge pillars soaring upward to be lost in a Cimmerian gloom!

Around me I saw grouped picturesquely in scattered order, and kneeling on their prie-dieux, the honest burghers, women and men, the former arrayed in the comfortable and not unpicturesque black Flemish cloaks with the silk hoods—handsome and effective garments, and almost universal. The devotional rite of the mass, deeply impressive, was over in twenty minutes, and all trooped away to their daily work. There was a suggestion here, in this modest, unpretending exercise, in contrast to the great fane itself, of the undeveloped power to expand, as it were, on Sundays and feast-days, when the cathedral would display all its resources, and its huge area be crowded to the doors with worshippers, and the great rites celebrated in all their full magnificence.

Behind the great altar I came upon an imposing monument, conceived after an original and comprehensive idea. It was to the memory of all the bishops and canons of the cathedral! This wholesale idea may be commended to our chapters at home. It might save the too monotonous repetition of recumbent bishops, who, after being exhibited at the Academy, finally encumber valuable space in their own cathedrals.

The suggestiveness of the great bell-tower, owing to the peculiar emphasis and purpose given to it, is constantly felt in the old Belgian cities. It still conveys its old antique purpose—the defence of the burghers, a watchful sentinel who, on the alarm, clanged out danger, the sound piercing from that eyry to the remotest lane, and bringing the valiant citizens rushing to the great central square. It is impossible to look up at one of these monuments, grim and solitary, without feeling the whole spirit of the Belgian history, and calling up Philip van Artevelde and the Ghentish troubles.

In the smaller cities the presence of this significant landmark is almost invariable. There is ever the lone and lorn tower, belfry, or spire painted in dark sad colours, seen from afar off, rising from the decayed little town below; often of some antique, original shape that pleases, and yet with a gloomy misanthropical air, as of total abandonment. They are rusted and abrased. From their ancient jaws we hear the husky, jangling chimes, musical and melancholy, the disorderly rambling notes and tunes of a gigantic musical box. Towards the close of some summer evening, as the train flies on, we see the sun setting on the grim walls of some dead city, and on the clustered houses. Within the walls are the formal rows of trees planted in regimental order which fringe and shelter them; while rises the dark, copper-coloured tower, often unfinished and ragged, but solemn and funereal, or else capped by some quaint lantern, from whose jaws presently issue the muffled tones of the chimes, halting and broken, and hoarse and wheezy with centuries of work. Often we pass on; sometimes we descend, and walk up to the little town and wander through its deserted streets. We are struck with wonder at some vast and noble church, cathedral-like in its proportions, and nearly always original—such variety is there in these antique Belgian fanes—and facing it some rustic mouldering town-hall of surprising beauty. There are a few little shops, a few old houses, but the generality have their doors closed. There is hardly a soul to be seen, certainly not a cart. There are innumerable dead cities of this pattern.

Coming out, I find it broad day. A few natives with their baskets are hurrying to the train. I note, rising above the houses, two or three other solemn spires and grim churches, which have an inexpressibly sad and abandoned air, from their dark grimed tones which contrast with the bright gay hues of the modern houses that crowd upon them. There is one grave, imposing tower, with a hood like a monk's. Then I wander to the handsome triangle-shaped place, with its statue to Margaret of Parma—erst Governor of the Netherlands, and whose memory is regarded with affection. Here is the old belfry, which has been so clamorous, standing apart, like those of Ghent, Dunkirk, and a few other towns; an effective structure, though fitted by modern restorers with an entirely new 'head'—not, however, ineffective of its kind.

The day is now fairly opened. There is a goodly muster of market-women and labourers at the handsome station, which, like every station of the first rank in Belgium, bears its name 'writ large.' It is just striking five as we hurry away, and in some half an hour we arrive at ORCHIES—one of those new spick-and-span little towns, useful after their kind, but disagreeable to the æsthetic eye. Everything here is of that meanest kind of brick, 'pointed,' as it is called, with staring white, such as it is seen in the smaller Belgian stations. Feeling somewhat degraded by this contact, I was glad to be hurried away, and within an hour find we are approaching one of the greater French cities.

VI.

DOUAI.

Now begin to flit past us signs unmistakable of an approaching fortified town. Here are significant green banks and mounds cut to angles and geometrical patterns, soft and enticing, enriched with luxuriant trees, but treacherous—smiling on the confiding houses and gardens which one day may be levelled at a few hours' notice. Next come compact masses of Vauban brick, ripe and ruddy, of beautiful, smooth workmanship; stately military gateways and drawbridges, with a patch of red trousering—a soldier on his fat Normandy 'punch' ambling lazily over; and the peaceful cart with its Flemish horses. The brick-work is sliced through, as with a cheese-knife, to admit the railway, giving a complete section of the work. We are, in short, at one of the great places fortes of France, Douai, where the curious traveller had best avoid sketching, or taking notes—a serious offence. Here I lingered pleasantly for nearly three hours, and, having duly breakfasted, noted its air of snug comfort and prosperity. There is here a famous arsenal—ever busy—one of the most important in France, and it has besides some welcome bits of artistic architecture.

It was when wandering down a darkish street, that I came on a most original building, the old Mairie, enriched with a belfry of delightfully graceful pattern. It might be a problem how to combine a bell-tower with offices for municipal work, and we know in our land how such a 'job' would be carried out by 'the architect to the Board.' But all over Flemish France and Belgium proper we find an inexhaustible fancy and fertility in such designs. It is always difficult to describe architectural beauties. This had its tower in the centre, flanked by two short wings. Everything was original—the disposition of the windows, the air of space and largeness. Yet the whole was small, I note that in all these Flemish bell-towers, the topmost portion invariably develops into something charmingly fantastic, into cupolas and short, little galleries and lanterns superimposed, the mixture of solidity and airiness being astonishing. It is appropriate and fitting that this grace should attend on what are the sweetest musical instruments conceivable. Mr. Haweis, who is the poet of Flemish bells, has let us into the secret. 'The fragment of aërial music,' he tells us, 'which floats like a heavenly sigh over the Belgian city and dies away every few minutes, seems to set all life and time to celestial music. It is full of sweet harmonies, and can be played in pianoforte score, treble and bass. After a week in a Belgian town, time seems dull without the music in the air that mingled so sweetly with all waking moods without disturbing them, and stole into our dreams without troubling our sleep. I do not say that such carillons would be a success in London. In Belgium the towers are high above the towns—Antwerp, Mechlin, Bruges—and partially isolated. The sound falls softly, and the population is not so dense as in London. Their habit and taste have accustomed the citizens to accept this music for ever floating in the upper air as part of the city's life—the most spiritual, poetical, and recreative part of it. Nothing of the kind has ever been tried in London. The crashing peals of a dozen large bells banged violently with clapper instead of softly struck with hammer, the exasperating dong, or ding, dong, of the Ritualist temple over the way, or the hoarse, gong-like roar of Big Ben—that is all we know about bells in London, and no form of church discipline could be more ferocious. Bell noise and bell music are two different things.' This fanciful tower had its four corner towerlets, suggesting the old burly Scotch pattern, which indeed came from France; while the vane on the top still characteristically flourishes the national Flemish lion.

Most bizarre, not to say extravagant, was the great cathedral, which was laid out on strange 'lines,' having a huge circular chapel or pavilion of immense height in front, whose round roof was capped by a vast bulbous spire, in shape something after the pattern of a gigantic mangel-wurzel! This astonishing decoration had a quaint and extraordinary effect, seen, as it was, from any part of the city. Next came the nave, whilst the transepts straggled about wildly, and a gigantic fortress-like tower reared itself from the middle. Correct judges will tell us that all this is debased work, and 'corrupt style;' but, nevertheless, I confess to being both astonished and pleased.

This was the great festival of the Corpus Domini, and, indeed, already all available bells in the place had been jangling noisily. It was now barely seven o'clock, yet on entering the vast nave I found that the 'Grand Mass' had begun, and the whole was full to the door, while in the great choir were ranged about a hundred young girls waiting to make their first Communion. A vast number of gala carriages were waiting at the doors to take the candidates home, and for the rest of the day they would promenade the city in their veils and flowers, receiving congratulations. There was a pleasant provincial simplicity in all this and in all that followed, which brought back certain old Sundays of a childhood spent on a hill overlooking Havre. I liked to see the stout red-cheeked choristers perspiring with their work, and singing with a rough stentoriousness, just as I had seen them in the village church of Sanvic. And there was the organist playing away at his raised seat in the body of the church, as if in a pew, visible to the naked eye of all; while two cantors in copes clapped pieces of wood together as a signal for the congregation to kneel or rise. Most quaint of all were the surpliced instrumentalists with their braying bassoon and ophicleide: not to forget the double-bass player who 'sawed' away for the bare life of him. The ever visible organist voluntarized ravishingly and in really fine style. I should like to have heard him at his own proper instrument, aloft, in the gallery yonder, quite an enormous structure of florid pipes in stories and groups, with angels blowing trumpets and flying saints. It seemed like the stern of one of the Armada vessels. How he would have made the pillars quiver! how the ripe old notes would have twanged and brayed into the darkest recesses!

The Mass being over, the Swiss, a tall, fierce fellow, arrayed in a feathered cocked-hat, rich scarlet regimentals and boots, now showed an extra restlessness. The Bishop of Douai, a smooth, polished prelate, began his sermon, which he delivered from a chair, in clear tones and good elocution. When the ceremonies were over, the whole congregation gathered at the door to see the young ladies taken away by their friends. Then I resumed my exploring.

On a cheerful-looking place, which, with its trees and kiosque, recalled the Place Verte at Antwerp, I noticed a large building of the pattern so common in France for colleges and convents—a vast expanse of whiteness or blankness, and a yet vaster array of long windows. It appeared to be a cavalry barrack for soldiers. The bugles sounded through the archway, and orderlies were riding in and out. This monotonous building, I found, had once been the English college for priests, where the celebrated Douai or Douay Bible had been translated. This rare book—a joy for the bibliophile—was published about 1608, and, as is well known, was the first Catholic version in English of the Scriptures. Here, then, was the cradle of millions of copies distributed over the face of the earth. It was a curious sensation to pass by this homely-looking edifice, with the adjoining chapel, as it appeared to be—now apparently a riding-school. I also came upon many a fine old Spanish house, and toiled down in the sun to the Rue des Foulons, where there were some elaborate specimens.

Short as had been my term of residence, I somehow seemed to know Douai very well. I had gathered what is called 'an idea of the place.' Its ways, manners, and customs seemed familiar to me. So I took my way from the old town with a sort of regret, having seen a great deal.

VII.

ARRAS.

It is just eleven o'clock, and here we are coming to a charming town, which few travellers have probably visited, and of which that genial and experienced traveller, Charles Dickens, wrote in astonished delight, and where in 1862 he spent his birthday. 'Here I find,' he says, 'a grand place, so very remarkable and picturesque, that it is astonishing how people miss it.' This is old Arras; and I confess it alone seems worth a long day's, not to say night's, journey, to see. It is fortified, and, as in such towns, we have to make our way to it from the station by an umbrageous country road; for it is fenced, as a gentleman's country seat might be, and strictly enclosed by the usual mounds, ditches, and walls, but all so picturesquely disguised in rich greenery as to be positively inviting. Even low down in the deep ditches grew symmetrical avenues of straight trees, abundant in their leaves and branches, which filled them quite up. The gates seem monumental works of art, and picturesque to a degree; while over the walls—and what noble specimens of brickwork, or tiling rather, are these old Vauban walls!—peep with curious mystery the upper stories and roofs of houses with an air of smiling security. I catch a glimpse of the elegant belfry, the embroidered spires, and mosque-like cupolas, all a little rusted, yet cheerful-looking. Dickens's place, or two places rather—for there is the greater and the less—display to us a really lovely town-hall in the centre, the roof dotted over with rows of windows, while an airy lace-work spire, with a ducal crown as the finish, rises lightly. On to its sides are encrusted other buildings of Renaissance order, while behind is a mansion still more astonishingly embroidered in sculptured stone, with a colonnade of vast extent. Around the place itself stretches a vast number of Spanish mansions, with the usual charmingly 'escalloped' roof, all resting on a prolonged colonnade or piazza, strange, old-fashioned, and original, running round to a vast extent, which the sensible town has decreed is never to be interfered with. A more pleasing, refreshing, and novel collection of objects for the ordinary traveller of artistic taste to see without trouble or expense, it would be impossible to conceive. Yet everyone hurries by to see the somewhat stale glories of Ghent and Brussels.

There was a general fat contented air of bourgeois comfort about the sleepy old-fashioned, handsome Prefecture—in short, a capital background for the old provincial life as described by Balzac. But the place, with its inimitable Spanish houses and colonnades—under which you can shop—and that most elegant of spires, sister to that of Antwerp, which it recalls, will never pass from the memory. A beautiful object of this kind, thus seen, is surely a present, and a valuable one too.

A spire is often the expression of the whole town. How much is suggested by the well-known, familiar cathedral spire at Antwerp, as, of some fresh morning, we come winding up the tortuous Scheldt, the sad, low-lying plains and boulders lying on either hand, monotonous and dispiriting, yet novel in their way; the cream-coloured, lace-worked spire rising ever before us in all its elegant grace, pointing the way, growing by degrees, never for an instant out of sight. It seems a fitting introduction to the noble, historical, and poetical city to which it belongs. It is surely ANTWERP! We see Charles V., and Philip, and the exciting troubles of the Gueux, the Dutch, the Flemings, the argosies from all countries in the great days of its trade. Such is the mysterious power of association, which it ever exerts on the 'reminiscent.' How different, and how much more profitable, too, is this mode of approaching the place, than the other more vulgar one of the railway terminus, with the cabs and omnibuses waiting, and the convenient journey to the hotel.

These old cities—Lille, Douai, and Valenciennes—all boast their gateways, usually named after the city to which the road leads. Thus we have 'Porte de Paris,' 'Porte de Lille,' etc. I confess to a deep interest in all gateways of this kind; they have a sort of poetry or romance associated with them; they are grim, yet hospitable, at times and seasons having a mysterious suggestion. There are towns where the traveller finds the gate obdurately closed between ten o'clock at night and six in the morning. These old gates have a state and flamboyant majesty about them, as, in Lille, the Porte de Paris is associated with the glories of Louis XIV.; while in Douai there is one of an old pattern—it is said of the thirteenth century—with curious towers and spires. Even at Calais there is a fine and majestic structure,

'Porte de Richelieu,' on the town side, through which every market cart and carriage used to trundle. There are florid devices inscribed on it; but now that the walls on each side are levelled, this patriarchal monument has but a ludicrous effect, for it is left standing alone, unsupported and purposeless. The carts and tramcars find their way round by new and more convenient roads made on each side.

How pleasant is that careless wandering up through some strange and unfamiliar place, led by a sort of instinct which habit soon furnishes! In some of the French 'Guides,' minute directions are given for the explorer, who is bidden to take the street to right or to left, after leaving the station, etc. But there is a piquancy in this uncertainty as compared with the odious guidance of the laquais de place. I loathe the tribe. Here was to be clearly noted the languid, lazy French town where nothing seemed to be doing, but everyone appeared to be comfortable—'the fat, contented, stubble goose'—another type of town altogether from your thriving Lilles and Rouens.

The pleasure in surveying this extraordinary combination of beautiful objects, the richness and variety of the work, the long lines broken by the charming and, as they are called, 'escalloped' gables, the Spanish balconies, the pillars, light and shade, and shops, made it almost incredible that such a thing was to be found in a poor obscure French town, visited by but few travellers. On market-day, when the whole is filled up with country folks, their wares and their stalls sheltered from the sun by gaily-tinted awnings, the bustle and glinting colours, and general va et vient, impart a fitting dramatic air. Then are the old Spanish houses set off becomingly.

This old town has other curious things to exhibit, such as the enormous old Abbey of St. Vaast—with its huge expansive roof, which somehow seems to dominate the place, and thrusts forward some fragment or other—where a regiment might lodge. Its spacious gardens are converted to secular uses. Then I find myself at the old-new cathedral, begun about a century ago, and finished about fifty years since—a 'poorish' heartless edifice in the bald Italian manner, and quite unsuited to these old Flemish cities. I come out on a terrace with a huge flight of steps which leads to a lower portion of the city. This, indeed, leads down from the haute to the basse ville; and it is stated that a great portion of this upper town is supported upon catacombs or caves from which the white stone of the belfry and town-hall was quarried. It is a curious feeling to be shown the house in which Robespierre was born, which, for the benefit of the curious it may be stated, is to be found in the Rue des Rapporteurs, close to the theatre. Arras was a famous Jacobin centre, and from the balcony of this theatre, Lebon, one of the Jacobins, directed the executions, which took place abundantly on the pretty place.

Thus much, then, for Arras, where one would have liked to linger, nay, to stay a week or a few days. But this wishing to stay a week at a picturesque place is often a dangerous pitfall, as the amiable Charles Collins has shown in his own quaint style. Has anyone, he asks, ever, 'on arriving at some place he has never visited before, taken a sudden fancy to it, committed himself to apartments for a month certain, gone on praising the locality and all that belongs to it, ferreting out concealed attractions, attaching undue importance to them, undervaluing obvious defects: has he gone on in this way for three weeks,' or rather three days, 'out of his month, then suddenly broken down, found out his mistake, and pined in secret for deliverance?' So it would be, as I conceive, at Bruges, or perhaps at St. Omer. There you indeed appreciate the dead-alive city 'in all its quiddity.' But a few days in a 'dead-alive' city, were it the most picturesque in the world, would be intolerable.

By noon, when the sun has grown oppressively hot, I find myself set down at a sort of rural town, once flourishing, and of some importance – Bethune. A mile's walk on a parched road led up the hill to this languishing, decayed little place. It had its forlorn omnibus, and altogether suggested the general desolation of, say, Peterborough. Had it remained in Flemish hands, it would now have been flourishing. I doubt if any English visitor ever troubles its stagnant repose. Yet it boasts its 'grand' place, imposing enough as a memorial of departed greatness, and, as usual, a Flemish relic, in the shape of a charming belfry and town-hall combined. It was really truly 'fantastical' from the airiness of its little cupolas and galleries, and was in tolerable order. Like the old Calais watch-tower, it was caked round by, and embedded in, old houses, and had its four curious gargoyles still doing work.

On this 'grand' place I noticed an old house bearing date '1625,' and some wonderful feats in the way of red-tiled roofing, of which there were enormous stretches, all narrow, sinuous, and suggesting Nuremberg. I confess to having spent a rather weary hour here, and sped away by the next train.

VIII.

LILLE.

Two o'clock. We are on the road again; the sun is shining, and we are speeding on rapidly—changing from Flanders to France—which is but an hour or so away. Here the bright day is well forward. Now the welcome fat Flemish country takes military shape, for here comes the scarp, the angled ditch, the endless brick walling and embankment—a genuine fortified town of the first class—LILLE. Here, too, many travellers give but a glance from the window and hurry on. Yet an interesting place in its way. Its bright main streets seem as gay and glittering as those of Paris, with the additional air of snug provincial comfort. To one accustomed for months to the solemn sobriety of our English capital, with its work-a-day, not to say dingy look, nothing is more exhilarating or gay than one of these first-class French provincial towns, such as Marseilles, Bordeaux, or this Lille. There is a glittering air of substantial opulence, with an attempt—and a successful one—at fine boulevards and fine trees.

The approach to Lille recalled the protracted approach to some great English manufacturing town, the tall chimneys flying by the carriage-windows a good quarter of an hour before the town was reached. A handsome, rich, and imposing city, though content to accept a cast-off station from Paris, as a poor relative would accept a cast-off suit of clothes. The fine façade was actually transported here stone by stone, and a much more imposing one erected in its place.

The prevailing one-horse tram-cars seem to suit the Flemish associations. The Belgians have taken kindly and universally to them, and find them to be 'exactly in their way.' The fat Flemish horse ambles along lazily, his bells jingling. No matter how narrow or winding the street, the car threads its way. The old burgher of the Middle Ages might have relished it. The old disused town-hall is quaint enough with its elaborately-carved façade, with a high double roof and dormers, and a lantern surmounting all. A bit of true 'Low-Countries' work; but one often forgets that we are in French Flanders. Entertaining hours could be spent here with profit, simply in wandering from spot to spot, eschewing the 'town valet' and professional picture guide. It is an extraordinary craze, by the way, that our countrymen will want always 'to see the pictures,' as though that were the object of travelling.

One gazes with pleasure and some surprise at its handsome streets, where everyone seems to live and thrive. There is a general air of opulence. The new streets, built under the last empire on the Paris model, offer the same rich and effective detail of gilded inscriptions running across the houses, balconies and flowers, with the luxurious cafés below, and languid flaneurs sitting down to their absinthe or coffee among the orange-trees. These imposing mansions, built with judicious loans—the 'OBLIGATIONS OF THE CITY OF LILLE' are quoted on the Exchanges—are already dark and rusted, and harmonize with the older portions. At every turn there is a suggestion of Brussels, and nowhere so much as on the fine place, where the embroidered old Spanish houses aforesaid are abundant.

The old cathedral, imposing with its clustered apses and great length and loftiness, and restored façade, would be the show of any English town. The Lillois scarcely appreciate it, as a few years ago they ordered a brand-new one from 'Messrs. Clutton and Burgess, of London,' not yet complete, and not very striking in its modern effects and decorations. These vast old churches of the fourth or fifth class are always imposing from their size and pretensions and elaborateness of work, and are found in France and Belgium almost by the hundred. And so I wander on through the showy streets, thinking what stirring scenes this complacent old city has witnessed, what tale of siege and battle—Spaniard, Frenchman, and Fleming, Louis the Great, the refuge of Louis XVIII. after his flight. All the time there is the pleasant musical jangle going on of tramcars below and bell-chimes aloft. But of all things in Lille, or indeed elsewhere, there is nothing more striking than the old Bourse—the great square venerable block, blackened all over with age, its innumerable windows, high roof, and cornices, all elaborately and floridly wrought in decayed carvings. With this dark and venerable mass is piquantly contrasted the garish row of glittering shops filled with gaudy wares which forms the lowest story. Within is the noble court with a colonnade of pillars and arches in the florid Spanish style; in the centre a splendid bronze statue of the First Napoleon in his robes, which is so wrought as to harmonize admirably with the rest. In the same congenial spirit—a note of Belgian art which is quite unfamiliar to us—the walls of the colonnade are decorated with memorials of famous 'Stock Exchange' worthies and merchants, and nothing could be more skilful than the enrichment of these conventional records, which are made to harmonize by florid rococo decorations with the Spanish genre and encrusted with bronzes and marbles. This admirable and original monument is in itself worth a journey to see.

Who has been at Commines? though we are all familiar enough with the name of Philip of 'that ilk.' I saw how patriarchal life must be at Commines from a family repairing thither, who filled the whole compartment. This was a lady arrayed in as much jet-work as she could well carry, and who must have been an admirable femme de ménage, for she brought with her three little girls, and two obstreperous boys who kept saying every minute 'maman!' in a sort of whine or expostulation, and two aides-de-camp maids in spotless fly-away caps. With these assistants she was on perfect terms, and the maids conversed with her and dissented from her opinions on the happiest terms of equality. When taking my ticket I was asked to say would I go to Commines in France or to Commines in Belgium, for it seems that, by an odd arrangement, half the town is in one country and half in the other! Each has a station of its own. This curious partition I did not quite comprehend at first, and I shall not forget the indignant style in which, on my asking 'was this the French Commines,' I was answered that 'of course it was Commines in Belgium.' Here was yet another piquant bell-tower seen rising above trees and houses, long before we even came near to it. I was pursued by these pretty monuments, and I could hear this one jangling away musically yet wheezily.

It is past noon now as we hurry by unfamiliar stations, where the invariable abbé waits with his bundle or breviary in hand, or peasant women with baskets stand waiting for other trains. There is a sense of melancholy in noting these strange faces and figures—whom you thus pass by, to whom you are unknown, whom you will never see again, and who care not if you were dead and buried. (And why should they?) Then we hurry away northwards.

IX.

YPRES.

As the fierce heat of the sun began to relax and the evening drew on—it was close on half-past six o'clock—we found ourselves in Belgium once more. Suddenly, on the right, I noted, with some trees interposed, a sort of clustered town with whitened buildings, which suggested forcibly the view of an English cathedral town seen from the railway. The most important of the group was a great tower with its four spires. I knew instinctively that this was the famous old town-hall, the most astonishing and overpowering of all Belgian monuments.

Here we halted half an hour. The sun was going down; the air was cool; and there was that strange tinge of sadness abroad, with which the air seems to be charged towards eventide, as we, strangers and pilgrims in a foreign country, look from afar off at some such unfamiliar objects. There were a number of Flemings here returning from some meeting where they had been contending at their national game—shooting at the popinjay. Near to every small town and village I passed, I had noted an enormously tall white post with iron rods projecting at the top. This was the target, and it was highly amusing and characteristic to watch these burghers gathered round and firing at the bird or some other object on the top. Now they were all returning carrying their bows, and in high good-humour. A young and rubicund priest was of the party, regarded evidently with affection and pride by his companions; for all that he seemed to say and do was applauded, and greeted with obstreperous Flemish laughter. When an old woman came to offer cakes from her basket for sale, he convulsed his friends by facetious remarks as he made his selection from the basket, depreciating or criticizing their quality with sham disgust, delighting none so much as the venerable vendor herself. Every one wore a curious black silk cap, as a gala headpiece.

When they had gone their way, I set off on mine up to the old town. The approach was encouraging. A grand sweep faced me of old walls, rusted, but stout and vigorous, with corner towers rising out of a moat; then came a spacious bridge leading into a wide, encouraging-looking street of sound handsome houses. But, strange! not a single cab, restaurant, or hotel—nay, hardly a soul to be seen, save a few rustics in their blouses! It was all dead! I walked on, and at an abrupt turn emerged on the huge expanse of the place, and was literally dumbfoundered.

Now, of all the sights that I have ever seen, it must be confessed that this offered the greatest surprise and astonishment. It was bewildering. On the left spread away, almost a city itself, the vast, enormous town-hall—a vista of countless arches and windows, its roof dotted with windows, and so deep, expansive, and capacious that it alone seemed as though it might have lodged an army. In the centre rose the enormous square tower—massive—rock-like—launching itself aloft into Gothic spires and towers. All along the sides ran a perspective of statues and carvings. This astonishing work would take some minutes of brisk motion to walk down from end to end. It is really a wonder of the world, and, in the phrase applied to more ordinary things, 'seemed to take your breath away.' It is the largest, longest, most massive, solid, and enduring thing that can be conceived.

It has been restored with wonderful care and delicacy. By one of the bizarre arrangements—not uncommon in Flanders—a building of another kind, half Italian, with a round arched arcade, has been added on at the corner, and the effect is odd and yet pleasing. Behind rises a grim crag of a cathedral—solemn and mysterious—adding to the effect of this imposing combination, a sort of gloomy shadow overhanging all. The church, on entering, is found overpowering and original of its kind, with its vast arches and massive roof of groined stone. Truly an astonishing monument! The worst of such visits is that only a faint impression is left: and to gather the full import of such a monument one should stay for a few days at least, and grow familiar with it. At first all is strange. Every portion claims attention at once; but after a few visits the grim old monument seems to relax and become accessible; he lets you see his good points and treasures by degrees. But who could live in a Dead City, even for a day? Having seen these two wonders, I tried to explore the place, which took some walking, but nothing else was to be found. Its streets were wide, the houses handsome—a few necessary shops; but no cabs—no tramway—no carts even, and hardly any people. It was dead—all dead from end to end. The strangest sign of mortality, however, was that not a single restaurant or house of refection was to be found, not even on the spacious and justly called Grande Place! One might have starved or famished without relief. Nay, there was hardly a public-house or drinking-shop.

However, the great monument itself more than supplied this absence of vitality. One could never be weary of surveying its overpowering proportions, its nobility, its unshaken strength, its vast length, and flourishing air. Yet how curious to think that it was now quite purposeless, had no meaning or use! Over four hundred feet long, it was once the seat of bustle and thriving business, for which the building itself was not too large. The hall on the ground seems to stretch from end to end. Here was the great mart for linens—the toiles flamandes—once celebrated over Europe. Now, desolate is the dwelling of Morna! A few little local offices transact the stunted shrunken local business of the place; the post, the municipal offices, each filling up two or three of the arches, in ludicrous contrast to the unemployed vastness of the rest. It has been fancifully supposed that the name Diaper, as applied to linens, was supplied by this town, which was the seat of the trade, and Toile d'Ypres might be supposed, speciously enough, to have some connection with the place.

X.

BERGUES.

But en route again, for the sands are fast running out. Old fortified towns, particularly such as have been protected by 'the great Vauban,' are found to be a serious nuisance to the inhabitants, however picturesque they may seem to the tourist; for the place, constricted and wrapped in bandages, as it were, cannot expand its lungs. Many of the old fortressed towns, such as Ostend, Courtrai, Calais, have recently demolished their fortifications at great cost and with much benefit to themselves. There is something picturesque and original in the first sight of a place like Arras, or St. Omer, with the rich and lavish greenery, luxuriant trees, banks of grass by which the 'fosse' and grim walls are masked. Others are of a grim and hostile character, and show their teeth, as it were.

Dunkirk, a fortress of the 'first class,' fortified on the modern system, and therefore to the careless spectator scarcely appearing to be fortified at all—is a place of such extreme platitude, that the belated wayfarer longs to escape almost as soon as he arrives. There is literally nothing to be seen. But a few miles away, there is to be found a place which will indemnify the disgusted traveller, viz., BERGUES. As the train slackens speed I begin to take note of rich green banks with abundant trees planted in files, such as Uncle Toby would have relished in his garden. There is the sound as of passing over a military bridge, with other tokens of the fortified town. There it lies—close to the station, while the invariable belfry and heavy church rise from the centre, in friendly companionship. I have noted the air of sadness in these lone, lorn monuments, which perhaps arises from the sense of their vast age and all they have looked down upon. Men and women, and houses, dynasties and invaders, and burgomasters, have all passed away in endless succession; but they remain, and have borne the buffetings of storms and gales and wars and tumults. As we turn out of the station, a small avenue lined with trees leads straight to the entrance. The bright snowy-looking place basks in the setting sun, while the tops of the red-tiled roofs seem to peep at us over the walls. At the end of the avenue the sturdy gateway greets us cheerfully, labelled 'Porte de Biene,' flanked by two short and burly towers that rise out of the water; while right and left, the old brick walls, red and rusted, stretch away, flanked by corner towers. The moat runs round the whole, filled with the usual stagnant water. I enter, and then see what a tiny compact little place it is—a perfect miniature town with many streets, one running round the walls; all the houses sound and compact and no higher than two stories, so as to keep snug and sheltered under the walls, and not draw the enemy's fire. The whole seems to be about the size of the Green Park at home, and you can walk right across, from gate to gate, in about three minutes. It is bright, and clean 'as a new pin,' and there are red-legged soldiers drumming and otherwise employed.

Almost at once we come on the place, and here we are rewarded with something that is worth travelling even from Dover to see. There stands the old church, grim, rusted, and weather-beaten, rising in gloomy pride, huge enough to serve a great town; while facing it is the belfry before alluded to, one of the most elegant, coquettish, and original of these always interesting structures. The amateur of Flemish architecture is ever prepared for something pleasing in this direction, for the variety of the belfries is infinite; but this specimen fills one with special delight. It rises to a great height in the usual square tower-shape, but at each corner is flanked by a quaint, old-fashioned tourelle or towerlet, while in the centre is an airy elegant lantern of wood, where a musical peal of bells, hung in rows, chimes all day long in a most melodious way. Each of these towerlets is capped by a long, graceful peak or minaret. This elegant structure has always been justly admired by the architect, and in the wonderful folio of etchings by Coney, done more than fifty years ago, will be found a picturesque and accurate sketch.

It seemed a city of the dead. Now rang out the husky tinkling of the chimes which never flag, as in all Flemish cities, day or night. It supplies the lack of company, and has a comforting effect for the solitary man. From afar off comes occasionally the sound of the drum or the bugle, fit accompaniment for such surroundings. At the foot of the belfry was an antique building in another style, with a small open colonnade, which, though out of harmony, was still not inappropriate. The only thing jarring was a pretentious modern town-hall, in the style of one of our own vestry buildings, 'erected out of the rates,' and which must have cost a huge sum. It was of a genteel Italian aspect, so it is plain that French local administrators are, in matters of taste, pretty much as such folk are with us. One could have lingered long here, looking at this charming and graceful work, which its surroundings became quite as much as it did its surroundings.

While thus engaged it was curious to find that not a soul crossed the place. Indeed, during my whole sojourn in the town, a period of about half an hour, I did not see above a dozen people. There were but few shops; yet all was bright, sound, in good condition. There was no sign of decay or decaying; but all seemed to sleep. It was a French 'dead city.' But it surely lives and will live, by its remarkable bell tower, which at this moment is chiming away, with a melodious huskiness, its gay tunes, repeated every quarter of an hour, while as the hour comes round there breaks out a general and clamorous charivari.

XI.

ST. OMER.

After leaving this wonderful place, I was now speeding on once more back into France. In all these shifts and changes the douanier farce was carefully gone through. I was regularly invited to descend, even though baggageless, and to pass through the searching-room, making heroic protest as I did so that 'I had nothing to declare.' It was easy to distinguish the two nations in their fashion of performing this function, the French taking it au sérieux, and going through it histrionically, as it were; the Belgian being more careless and good-natured. There lingers still the habit of 'leading' or plombé-ing a clumsy, troublesome relic of old times. Such small articles as hat-cases, hand-bags, etc., are subjected to it; an officer devoted to the duty comes with a huge pair of 'pincers' with some neat little leaden discs, which he squeezes on the strings which have tied up the article.

Now we fly past the flourishing Poperinghe—a bustling, thriving place, out of which lift themselves with sad solemnity a few tall iron-gray churches, and another—yet one more—elegant belfry. There seems something quaint in the name of Poperinghe, though it is hardly so grotesque as that of another town I passed by, 'Bully Greny.'

As this long day was at last closing in, I noticed from the window a bright-looking town nestling, as it were, in rich green velvet and dark plantation, with a bright, snug-looking gate, drawbridge, etc. One of these gates was piquant enough, having a sort of pavilion perched on the top. Here there was a quaint sort of 'surprise' in a clock, the hours of which are struck by a mechanical figure known to the town as 'Mathurin.' There was something very tempting in the look of the place, betokening plenty of flowers and shaded walks and umbrageous groves. Most conspicuous, however, was the magnificent abbey ruin, suggesting Fountains Abbey, with its tall, striking, and wholly perfect tower. This is the Abbey of St. Bertin, one of the most striking and almost bewildering monuments that could be conceived. I look up at the superb tower, sharp in its details, and wonder at its fine proportions; then turn to the ruined aisles, and with a sort of grief recall that this, one of the wonders of France, had been in perfect condition not a hundred years ago, and at the time of the Revolution had been stripped, unroofed, and purposely reduced to its present condition! This disgrace reflects upon the Jacobins—Goths and Vandals indeed.

The streets of this old town, as it is remarked by one of the Guide Books, 'want animation'—an amiable circumlocution. Nothing so deserted or lonely can be conceived, and the phenomenon of 'grass literally growing in the streets' is here to be seen in perfection. There appeared to be no vehicles, and the few shops carry on but a mild business. A few English families are said to repair hither for economy. I recognise a peculiar shabby shooting-coat which betokens the exile, accounted for by the pathetic fact that he clings to his superannuated garment, long after it is worn out, for the reason that it 'was made in London.' There is a rich and beautiful church here—Notre Dame—with a deeply embayed porch full of lavish detail. Here, too, rises the image of John Kemble, who actually studied for the priesthood at the English College.

By this time the day has gone, and darkness has set in. It is time to think of journeying home. Yet on the way to Calais there are still some objects to be seen en passant. Most travellers are familiar with Hazebrouck, the place of 'bifurcation,' a frontier between France and Belgium. Yet this is known for a church with a most elegant spire rising from a tower, but of this we can only have a glimpse. And, on the road to Bergues, I had noted that strange, German-named little town—Cassel—perched on an umbrageous hill, which has its quaint mediæval town-hall. But I may not pause to study it. The hours are shrinking; but little margin is left. By midnight I am back in Calais once more, listening to its old wheezy chimes. It seems like an old friend, to which I have returned after a long, long absence, so many events have been crowded into the day. It still wants some interval to the hour past midnight, when the packet sails.

XII.

ST. PIERRE LES CALAIS.

As I wandered down to the end of the long pier, which stretched out its long arm, bent like an elbow, looking, like all French piers, as if made of frail wickerwork, I thought of a day, some years ago, when that eminent inventor, Bessemer, conceived the captivating idea of constructing a steamboat that should abolish sea-sickness for ever! The principle was that of a huge swinging saloon, moved by hydraulic power, while a man directed the movement by a sort of spirit-level. Previously the inventor had set up a model in his garden, where a number of scientists saw the section of a ship rocking violently by steam. I recall that pleasant day down at Denmark Hill, with all the engineers assembled, who were thus going to sea in a garden. A small steam-engine worked the apparatus—a kind of a section of a boat—which was tossed up and down violently; while in the centre was balanced a small platform, on which we experimenters stood. On large tables were laid out the working plans of the grand Bessemer steamship, to be brought out presently by a company.

A year and more passed away, the new vessel was completed, and nearly the same party again invited to see the result, and make trial of it. I repaired with the rest. Nothing more generous or hospitable could be conceived. There was to be a banquet at Calais, with a free ticket on to Paris. It was a gloomy iron-gray morning. The strange outlandish vessel, which had an engine at each end, was crowded with connoisseurs. But I was struck with the figure of the amiable and brilliant inventor, who was depressed, and received the premature congratulations of his friends somewhat ruefully. We could see the curious 'swinging saloon' fitted into the vessel, with the ingenious hydraulic leverage by which it could be kept nicely balanced. But it was to be noted that the saloon was braced firmly to the sides of its containing vessel; in fact, it was given out that, owing to some defect in its mechanism, the thing could not be worked that day. Nothing could be handsomer than this saloon, with its fittings and decorations. But, strange to say, it was at once seen that the principle was faulty, and the whole impracticable. It was obvious that the centre of

46

gravity of so enormous a weight being brought to the side would imperil the stability of the vessel. The bulk to be moved was so vast, that it was likely to get out of control, and scarcely likely to obey the slight lever which worked it. There were many shakings of the engineering heads, and some smiles, with many an 'I told you so.' Even to the outsiders it seemed Utopian.

However, the gloomy voyage was duly made. One of the most experienced captains known on the route, Captain Pittock, had been chosen to pilot the venture. He had plainly a distrust of his charge and the new-fangled notion. Soon we were nearing Calais. Here was the lighthouse, and here the two embracing arms of the wickerwork pier. I was standing at the bows, and could see the crowds on the shore waiting. Suddenly, as the word was given to starboard or 'port,' the malignant thing, instead of obeying, took the reverse direction, and bore straight into the pier on the left! Down crashed the huge flag-staff of our vessel in fragments, falling among us—and there were some narrow escapes. She calmly forced her way down the pier for nearly a hundred yards, literally crunching and smashing it up into fragments, and sweeping the whole away. I looked back on the disastrous course, and saw the whole clear behind us! As we gazed on this sudden wreck, I am ashamed to say there was a roar of laughter, for never was a surprise of so bewildering a character sprung upon human nature. The faces of the poor captain and his sailors, who could scarcely restrain their maledictions on the ill-conditioned 'brute,' betrayed mortification and vexation in the most poignant fashion. The confusion was extraordinary. She was now with difficulty brought over to the other pier. This, though done ever so gently, brought fresh damage, as the mere contact crunched and dislocated most of the timbers. The ill-assured party defiled ashore, and we made for the banqueting-room between rows of half-jeering, half-sympathizing spectators. The speakers at the symposium required all their tact to deal with the disheartening subject. The only thing to be done was to 'have confidence' in the invention—much as a Gladstonian in difficulty invites the world to 'leave all to the skill of our great chief.' But, alas! this would not do just now. The vessel was, in fact, unsteerable; the enormous weight of the engines at the bows prevented her obeying the helm. The party set off to Paris—such as were in spirits to do so—and the shareholders in the company must have had aching hearts enough.

Some years later, walking by the Thames bank, not far from Woolwich, I came upon some masses of rusted metal, long lying there. There were the huge cranks of paddle-wheels, a cylinder, and some boiler metal. These, I was informed, were the fragments of the unlucky steamship that was to abolish sea-sickness! As I now walked to the end of the solitary pier—the very one I had seen swept away so unceremoniously—the recollection of this day came back to me. There was an element of grim comedy in the transaction when I recalled that the Calais harbour officials sent in—and reasonably—a huge claim for the mischief done to the pier; but the company soon satisfied that by speedily going 'into liquidation.' There was no resource, so the Frenchmen had to rebuild their pier at their own cost.

Close to Calais is a notable place enough, flourishing, too, founded after the great war by one Webster, an English laceman. It has grown up, with broad stately streets, in which, it is said, some four or five thousand Britons live and thrive. As you walk along you see the familiar names, 'Smith and Co.,' 'Brown and Co.,' etc., displayed on huge brass plates at the doors in true native style. Indeed, the whole air of the place offers a suggestion of Belfast, these downright colonists having stamped their ways and manners in solid style on the place. Poor old original Calais had long made protest against the constriction she was suffering; the wall and ditch, and the single gate of issue towards the country, named after Richelieu, seeming to check all hope of improvement. Reasons of state were urged. But a few years ago Government gave way, the walls towards the country-side were thrown down, the ditch filled up, and some tremendous 'navigator' work was carried out. The place can now draw its breath.

On my last visit I had attended the theatre, a music-hall adaptable to plays, concerts, or to 'les meetings.' It was a new, raw place, very different from the little old theatre in the garden of Dessein's, where the famous Duchess of Kingston attended a performance over a hundred and twenty years ago.

This place bore the dignified title of the 'Hippodrome Theatre,' and a grand 'national' drama was going on, entitled

'THE CUIRASSIER OF REICHSHOFEN.'

Here we had the grand tale of French heroism and real victory, which an ungenerous foe persisted in calling defeat. A gallant Frenchman, who played the hero, had nearly run his daring course, having done prodigies of valour on that fateful and fatal day. The crisis of the drama was reached almost as I entered, the cuirassier coming in with his head bound up in a bloody towel! After relating the horrors of that awful charge in an impassioned strain, he wound up by declaring that 'He and Death' were the only two left upon the field! It need not be said there were abundant groans for the Germans and cheers for the glorious Frenchmen.

Now at last down to the vessel, as the wheezy chimes give out that it is close on two o'clock a.m. All seems dozing at 'Maritime Calais.' The fishing-boats lie close together, interlaced in black network, snoozing, as it were, after their labours. Afar off the little town still maintains its fortress-like air and its picturesque aspect, the dark central spires rising like shadows, the few lights twinkling. The whole scene is deliciously tranquil. The plashing of the water seems to invite slumber, or at least a temporary doze, to which the traveller, after his long day and night, is justly entitled. How strange those old days, when the exiles for debt abounded here! They were in multitudes then, and had a sort of society among themselves in this Alsatia. That gentleman in a high stock and a short-waisted coat—the late Mr. Brummell surely, walking in this direction? Is he pursued by this agitated crowd, hurrying after him with a low roaring, like the sound of the waves?...

I am roused up with a start. What a change! The whole is alive and bustling, black shadowy figures are hurrying by. The white-funnelled steamer has come up, and is moaning dismally, eager to get away. Behind is the long international train of illuminated chambers, fresh from Paris and just come in, pouring out its men and women, who have arrived from all quarters of the world. They stream on board in a shadowy procession, laden with their bundles. Lower down, I hear thecrashing of trunks discharged upon the earth! I go on board with the rest, sit down in a corner, and recall nothing till I find myself on the chill platform of Victoria Station—time, six o'clock a.m.

It was surely a dream, or like a dream!—a dream a little over thirty hours long. And what strange objects, all blended and confused together!—towers, towns, gateways, drawbridges, religious rites and processions, pealing organs and jangling chimes, long dusty roads lined with regimental trees, blouses, fishwomen's caps, sabots, savoury and unsavoury smells, France dissolving into Belgium, Belgium into France, France into Belgium again; in short, one bewildering kaleidoscope! A day and two nights had gone, during all which time I had been on my legs, and had travelled nigh six hundred miles! Dream or no dream, it had been a very welcome show or panorama, new ideas and sights appearing at every turn.

And here is my little 'orario':

	O'clock.
1. Victoria, depart	5.0
2. Dover, arrive	7.0
" depart	10.0
3. Calais, arrive	12.44
" depart	1.0
4. Tournay, arrive	4.13
" depart	5.1
5. Orchies, arrive	6.8
" depart	6.29
6. Douai, arrive	7.6
" depart	10.8
7. Arras, arrive	10.52
" depart	11.17

8. Bethune, arrive	12.6
" depart	1.1
9. Lille, arrive	2.44
" depart	4.40
10. Comines, arrive	5.19
" depart	5.57
11. Ypres	6.42
12. Hazebrouck	7.50
13. Cassel	8.18
14. Bergues, arrive	9.6
" depart	10.4
15. St. Omer	11.37
16. Calais	12.14
17. Dover	4.0
18. Victoria	6.0

Time on journey 37 hours

This, of course, is more than a day, but it will be seen that eight hours were spent on English soil, and certainly nearly twelve in inaction.

THE END.